Pua Pua Lena Lena

and the Magic Kiha-pu

An adaptation from the Hawaiian legends.

By Guy & Pam Buffet
Illustrated by Guy Buffet
Edited by Ruth Tabrah

An Island Heritage Book

Pua Pua Lena Lena and the Magic Kiha-pu
Written by Guy & Pam Buffet
Illustrated by Guy Buffet
Edited by Ruth Tabrah

Please address orders and
editorial correspondence to:
ISLAND HERITAGE PUBLISHING
A DIVISION OF THE MADDEN CORPORATION

99-880 Iwaena Street
Aiea, Hawaii 96701
Telephone (808) 487-7299

Second Edition, First Printing — 1994

In the days when Olopana was ruling Chief of Waipiʻo, there lived a Chiefess named Luʻukia.

Coconut palms shaded her hale near the sacred temple, Pakaʻalana. The valley was filled with her people, Hawaiians farming their taro and fishing in the sea.

Far back in the valley, the twin falls of Hiʻilawe thundered over the cliffs by Luʻukia's royal ʻawa patch. Tended by two loyal servants, Kekoa and Kamalu, the ʻawa patch grew no ordinary plants, but special ones with roots from which a drink of peace and happiness was brewed.

The dream of Chiefess Lu'ukia was to find where the 'uhane kept the conch trumpet, and return it to its rightful place in Paka'alana Heiau.

Then, Kiha-pu could once again be blown by those with mana. There would be sleep without fear in the valley of Waipi'o.

This had not always been so. Once chiefs and commoners slept every night knowing that the magic trumpet Kiha-pu, the conch shell of the ruling Chief Kiha, guarded them all.

Kiha-pu was a conch blown only by those with mana. It warned the chiefs and people of disaster. A tidal wave. The approach of an enemy. It summoned the aid of the gods when famine struck. It was the sacred treasure of Waipi'o, adorned with the teeth of the slain enemies of Kiha.

Sometimes Kiha-pu sounded like shrieks of warriors dying in battle. Sometimes it was like strong winds in the forest. Sometimes it shattered the peace of the valley like seas thundering against tall cliffs.

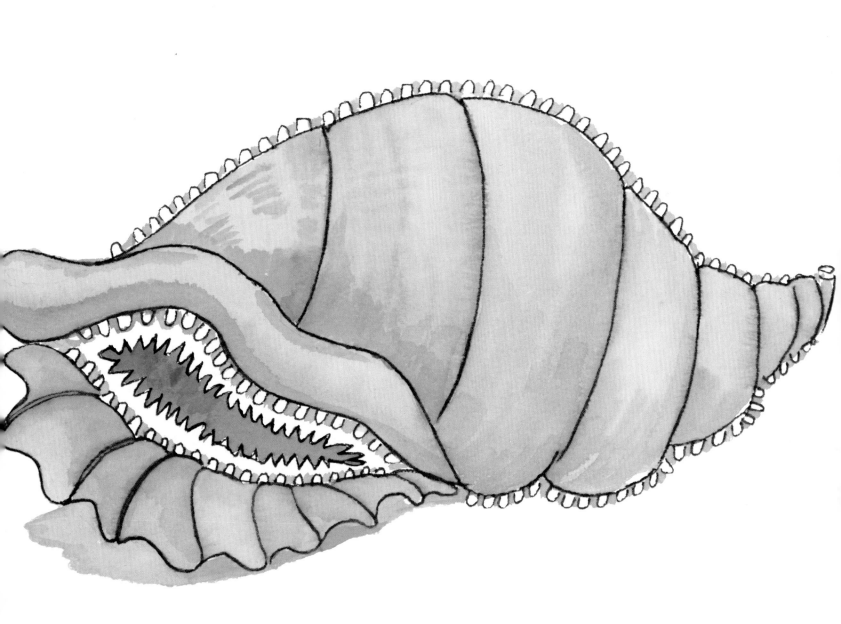

Before the birth of the Chiefess Lu'ukia, Waipi'o had lost its magic guardian. 'Uhane, the spirits of the night, had stolen Kiha-pu and taken it to a secret place.

Since then, neither chiefs nor villagers slept well. No one knew when the voice of Kiha-pu might jar their sleep with another 'uhane trick.

Once trusted by all, the sound of Kiha-pu was now dreaded by those who lived in the valley.

The valley was the most beautiful on the island of Hawaii. Chiefess Lu'ukia had lands and people loyal and loved by her. The images of the gods reared proud and fierce inside the stone walls of the heiau, Paka'alana.

Yet, Lu'ukia and her people were not happy. The valley of Waipi'o was an uneasy place.

One morning, Kekoa, one of the servants, was gathering 'awa for Lu'ukia and found that the choicest plants were gone.

He raced to tell her. Luʻukia was furious! She knew her people loved to drink ʻawa, but to steal from the royal ʻawa patch was punishable by death.

Night and day Kekoa and Kamalu guarded the ʻawa patch.

On the night of the full moon, a big white dog with brownish-yellow spots walked into the 'awa patch.

Skillfully, he stole the choicest of the 'awa plants.

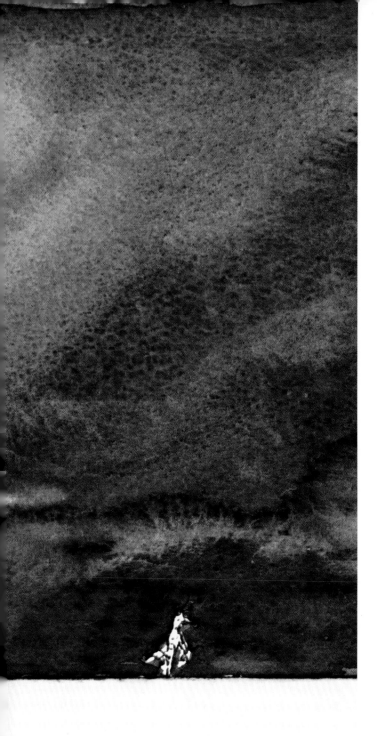

The dog raced down the valley to the beach. Spears in hand, Kekoa and Kamalu quietly followed.

When they reached the village of Honokohau, the dog disappeared into a small hale. Peering through the sides of the hale, Kekoa and Kamalu watched the dog prepare the 'awa root for drinking.

"This dog is Puapualenalena, the mysterious one," they whispered. "A *kupua*! There is nothing he cannot do!"

They watched as the dog served the 'awa to a bent old man sitting in the corner. His back was so crippled it seemed covered with hills and valleys. Over his misty eyes hung eyebrows like great pieces of thatch.

As the first sip was being taken, the men burst in!

Kekoa and Kamalu brought the two before Chiefess Luʻukia and told her the strange story.

Pointing to them she said..........

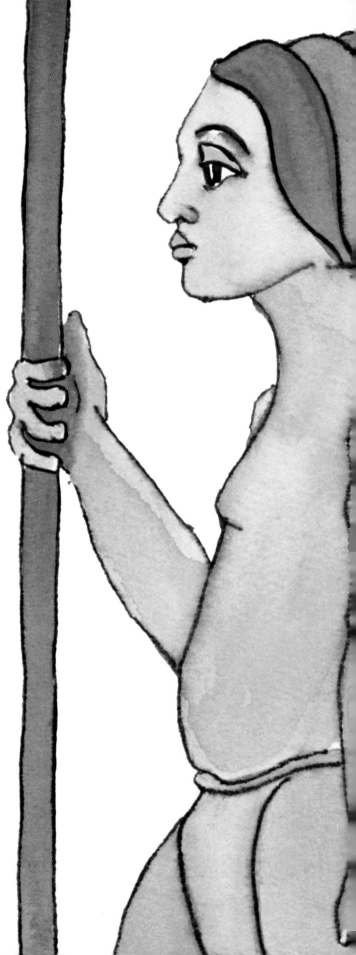

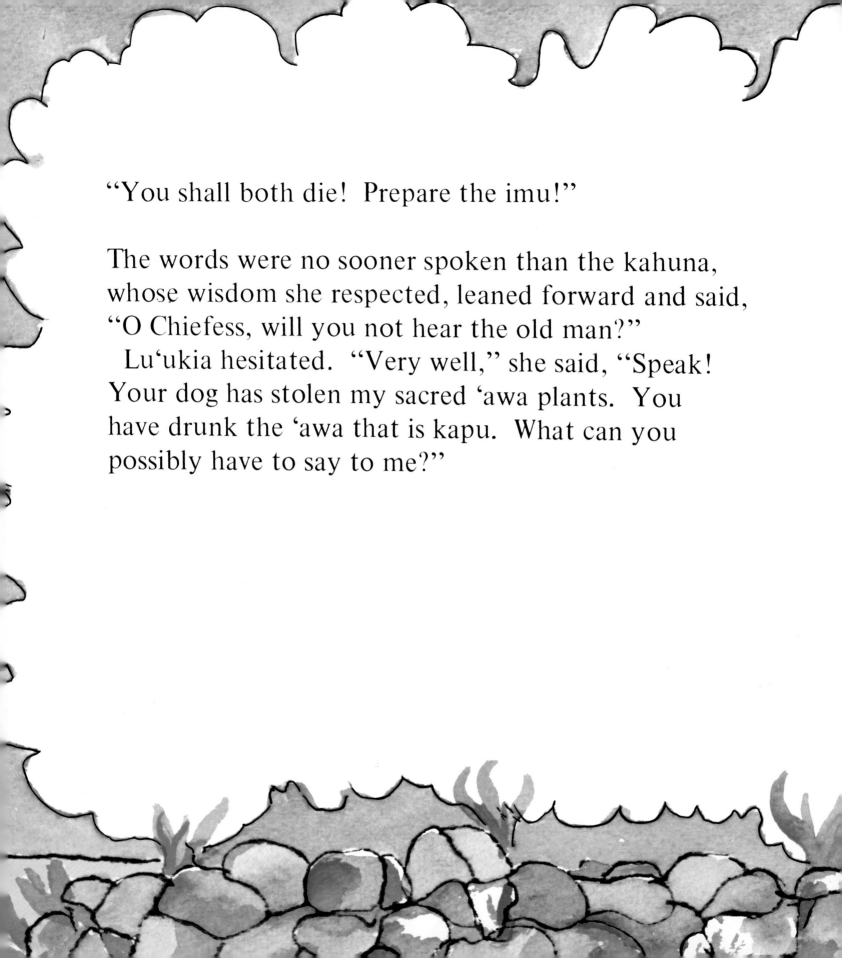

"You shall both die! Prepare the imu!"

The words were no sooner spoken than the kahuna, whose wisdom she respected, leaned forward and said, "O Chiefess, will you not hear the old man?"
    Lu'ukia hesitated. "Very well," she said, "Speak! Your dog has stolen my sacred 'awa plants. You have drunk the 'awa that is kapu. What can you possibly have to say to me?"

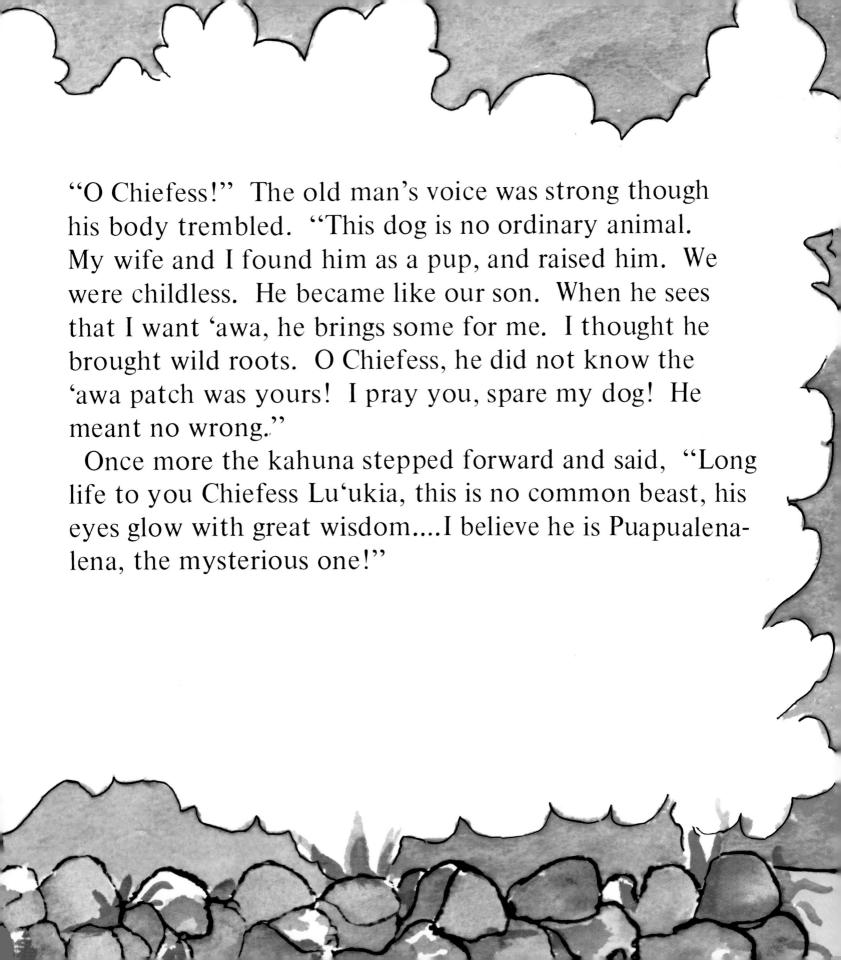

"O Chiefess!" The old man's voice was strong though his body trembled. "This dog is no ordinary animal. My wife and I found him as a pup, and raised him. We were childless. He became like our son. When he sees that I want 'awa, he brings some for me. I thought he brought wild roots. O Chiefess, he did not know the 'awa patch was yours! I pray you, spare my dog! He meant no wrong."

Once more the kahuna stepped forward and said, "Long life to you Chiefess Lu'ukia, this is no common beast, his eyes glow with great wisdom....I believe he is Puapualena-lena, the mysterious one!"

Looking into the dog's eyes Lu'ukia said, "Old man, if your dog can bring me Kiha-pu by morning, your lives will be spared."

The old man turned to Pua-pualenalena and said....

"Can you do this?"

Puapualenalena wagged his tail and with his eyes told the old man that he understood.

Puapualenalena made himself a kukui nut torch. He started up the trail from the valley to Kukuihaele.

"Auwe!" he panted at the top of the trail.
"How foolish, I should have made myself bigger. I could have made the climb in half the time!"

His wet nose sniffed the wind. In the distance, above a high rock wall, he saw the glow of a fire.

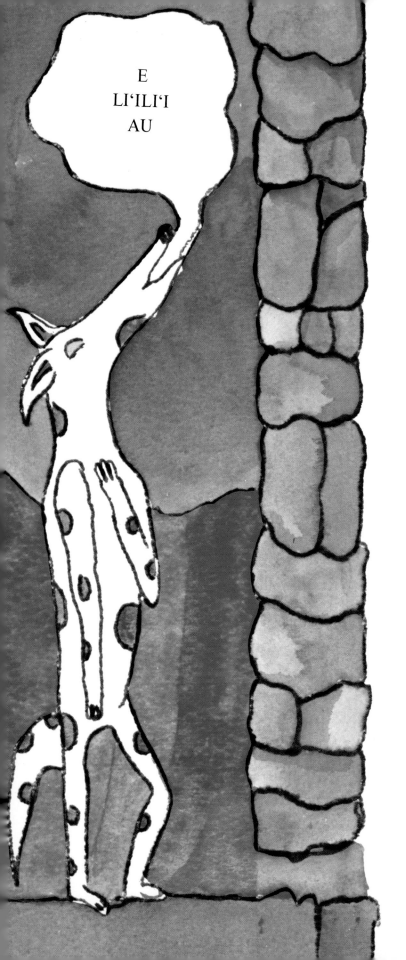

E
LI'ILI'I
AU

"This must be the secret place of the 'uhane. How can I get inside," thought Puapualenalena. "The entrance is closed with pulo'ulo'u."

"I could make myself tall and step over the wall, but surely they would see me."

Puapualenalena searched
until he found a small
hole between the stones
at the base of the wall.
"E liʻiliʻi au!....I am
small!" At once, he
became the size of a
mouse and wriggled
through a puka into
the ʻuhane camp.

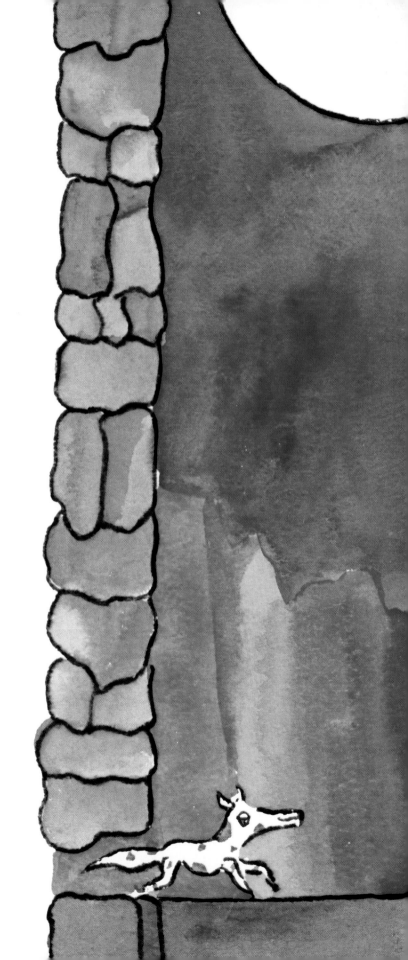

The ʻuhane were gathered around the fire plotting their next trick. Puapualenalena heard them talking about the magic conch shell. He was certain Kiha-pu must be inside the walls.

"If I am going to find Kiha-pu I must get them to fall asleep before dawn," thought Puapualenalena. "I'll change back to my own size. I'll start a dance contest. That should tire them out!"

Wagging his tail and shaking a pair of uli-uli, Puapualena-lena began to dance the hula. His dog teeth anklets clicked to the rhythm.

The 'uhane screamed with laughter. A dancing dog? No dog would outdance them! Soon they were dancing wildly, each trying to outlast the other.

It was dawn before the last of the 'uhane fell into exhausted sleep.

At the far end of the camp, Puapualenalena could see a bamboo tower. Atop it was an enormous conch shell.

KIHA-PU!

"I must hurry! Dawn is breaking. The imu awaits my master," said Puapualenalena. "E nui au! I am big!" At once he became thirty feet tall. He grabbed the shell in his strong teeth and hurried away.

In his haste, Puapualenalena tripped and fell.

Kiha-pu rolled down the trail ahead of him, sounding like thunder. The noise awakened the sleeping ʻuhane, who immediately saw that Kiha-pu was missing. But the sun had risen and the ʻuhane, creatures of the night, could not follow.

Kiha-pu tumbled down the trail so
fast that Puapualenalena could not
catch it.

   On and on the magic conch
rolled until it crashed into the
wall of the heiau.

The noise awakened everyone
in Waipi'o.

Puapualenalena changed himself back to his normal size. He stood proudly by Kiha-pu.

The Chiefess and her people were overjoyed. She freed the old man and favored them both with maile leis. "The choicest of my 'awa lands are yours," she said.

The sacred Kiha-pu was back in the heiau of Paka'alana.

From that day on.....

there was peace in Waipi'o Valley.

An Introduction to
Things Hawaiian

'AWA (a´va) - The plant piper methysticum. The root was used to brew a tranquilizing drink.

HALE (ha´le) - House. Usually built with sapling or bamboo frame, and thatched with pili grass. When grass was scarce, pandanus leaves were used.

HEIAU (hei´yau) - An open-air temple with stone paving and walls of carefully set stones.

HI'ILAWE (hi´'i-la´ve) - A spectacular water fall in Waipi'o. The name is widely known through a song composed about it.

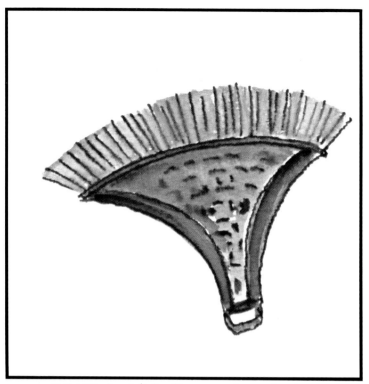

PE'AHI (pe-'a'hi) - Fan or to fan or beckon. In olden days fans were made both of coconut and pandanus or hala leaves and were often very ornamental.

LU'UKIA (lu-'u-ki'a) - Hawaiian chiefess who lived in Waipi'o Valley during the seventeenth century.

KUKUI NUT TORCHES (ku-kwi) - Nuts of the candle-nut tree, threaded on palm frond mid-rib and burned serially.

KUPUA (ku-pu'a) - A supernatural being with the power to change his size, shape or form. Puapualenalena, the dog in this story, was a kupua.

MAUNA KEA (maʻu-na keʻa) - Highest mountain in the islands (13,792 feet). It is on the island of Hawaiʻi, southeast of Waipiʻo and contains a long dormant volcano.

ʻUHANE (ʻu-haʻne) - Soul, spirit, ghost. Often however, ghost is called ʻuhane lapu - spirit which haunts.

ʻULIʻULI (ʻu-lee-ʻu-lee) - Feather topped gourd used as a rhythm instrument in the ʻuliʻuli dance.

WAIPIʻO (vai-piʻ-ʻo) - A beautiful valley on the Hamakua Coast of the island of Hawaiʻi. An important seat of culture in old Hawaiʻi.

IMU (iʻmu) - Underground earth oven in which food was cooked and, on rare occasions, people.

PULOʻULOʻU (poo-loʻ-ʻu-loʻ-ʻu) - Tapa ball on a stick, used as a sign or marker of prohibition. It was generally carried before a chief as insignia of kapu (ka-pu).

MORTAR AND PESTLE - Hollow stone container and pounder in varying sizes, used to crush or pound medicinal herbs and prepare some ingredients for dyes.

CHIEF KIHA (kiʻha) - A ruling chief of Waipiʻo on the island of Hawaiʻi in the sixteenth century.

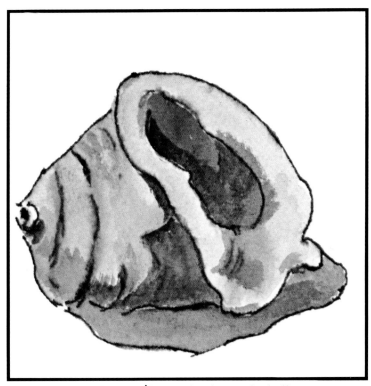

KIHA-PU (ki′ha-poo) - A conch shell adorned with human teeth, once owned by Chief Kiha, now in the Bishop Museum in Honolulu.

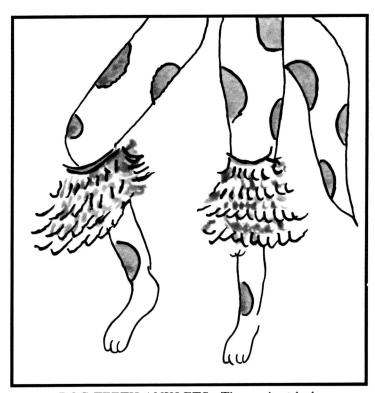

DOG TEETH ANKLETS - The ancient hula was danced by men as well as women. Dog teeth anklets were part of the traditional male dance costume.

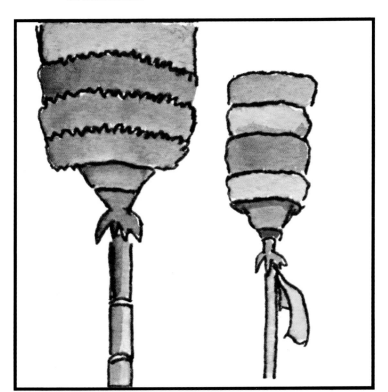

KAHILI (kah-hi′li) - Royal standard symbolic of royalty, made of feathers fastened to a net base at the top of a long pole.

KI′I AKUA (ki′-′i a-ku′a - link the i and a) Images of gods made of wickerwork covered with feathers or carved out of wood or stone.